Billy Porter

A Little Golden Book® Biography

By Phil Stamper
Illustrated by Steffi Walthall

 A GOLDEN BOOK • NEW YORK

Golden Books
An imprint of Random House Children's Books • A division of Penguin Random House LLC
1745 Broadway, New York, NY 10019 • penguinrandomhouse.com • rhcbooks.com
Text copyright © 2025 by Phil Stamper
Cover art and interior illustrations copyright © 2025 by Steffi Walthall
Golden Books, A Golden Book, A Little Golden Book, the G colophon, and the distinctive
gold spine are registered trademarks of Penguin Random House LLC.
Library of Congress Control Number: 2024945103
ISBN 978-0-593-89810-9 (trade) — ISBN 978-0-593-89811-6 (ebook)
Manufactured in the United States of America
10 9 8 7 6 5 4 3 2 1
EU Contact: Penguin Random House Ireland, 32 Nassau Street, Dublin D02 YH68.
https://eu-contact.penguin.ie.

Billy Porter was born William Ellis Porter II on September 21, 1969, in Pittsburgh, Pennsylvania. He and his younger sister were raised by their loving mother in a very religious family.

Growing up in the Black church community, he fell in love with gospel music and fashion. Every Sunday seemed like a fashion show to him. Billy saw that clothes were the perfect way to stand out and let people know who you are.

As a kid, Billy didn't care much for sports, but he loved playing jacks and double Dutch with the girls on the playground. Billy felt like he acted more feminine than the other boys in his school, and he was bullied a lot for it.

But when he sang at the school talent show in fifth grade, everyone was wowed by his voice. He used his passion for singing to stand up to his bullies.

Billy always knew he was a star. After that day, everyone else knew it, too!

For his eleventh birthday, Billy's grandmother took him to the musical *The Wiz*. Seeing people who looked like him singing and dancing on the stage made an impact that would stay with him forever.

The next year, Billy was washing dishes and watching TV. The Tony Awards—a ceremony that celebrates the best plays and musicals on Broadway— caught his attention. An actress named Jennifer Holliday was singing a song from *Dreamgirls*.

The performance took Billy's breath away. He decided right then that he would spend his life performing, making audiences feel as inspired as he did in that moment.

In middle school, Billy joined an after-school program for musical theater. He studied music, joined a choir, and took dance lessons. He knew he had the skills to be one of the best entertainers of all time, and he wouldn't stop until he achieved his goal.

When he was fifteen, Billy got a special summer job. He was hired as a performer at an amusement park near his hometown!

He sang and danced in six shows a day, six days a week, for the entire summer. Billy was making money doing what he loved. His dream was starting to come true.

Billy's singing and dancing were getting better and better, but to be a musical theater star, he would need to know how to act, too. He got a full scholarship to the Carnegie Mellon University School of Drama, where he learned everything about being onstage— even how to build sets and sew costumes!

College wasn't easy, but he and his classmates always had fun. They loved throwing big parties to watch the Oscars, an award show for actors and moviemakers.

Before the ceremony, the guests posed on the red carpet. Billy was tired of seeing all the men wearing boring suits. He promised his friends he would wear a fancy gown when he got invited to the Oscars one day.

While he was in college, Billy spent his summers going to auditions in New York City. He was hoping to get a part in a Broadway show. Unfortunately, he kept hearing no.

When he was twenty-one, he auditioned for *Miss Saigon* and finally heard yes. After years of hard work, Billy was going to sing, dance, and act on Broadway for the first time!

Billy also
performed on TV.

He competed against other singers on the talent
show *Star Search* and won the Male Vocalist category!

A few years later, he released his first R & B album and made music videos for his songs. Even though he loved making music, Billy was sad. The record company told him to hide his true self—they wouldn't let him talk about being on Broadway, and they made him sing love songs about girls.

After nearly a year in *Miss Saigon*, he worked on a few other Broadway shows. Billy was excited when he got the role of Teen Angel in *Grease*, but the costume he had to wear just made him feel like a clown.

Billy spent ten years on Broadway, but still had a hard time finding roles for people who looked like him. Eventually, he made the difficult decision to take a break from acting. He focused on writing and teaching instead.

Thirteen years later, Billy heard that *Kinky Boots*, a movie about a factory that made dazzling shoes for drag performers, was being turned into a musical. The story of *Kinky Boots* is about accepting others for who they are. And the main character, Lola, was a confident Black drag queen. This was exactly the kind of role and show Billy had been looking for.

After months of auditions, Billy got the role of a lifetime. He was heading back to Broadway!

In 2013, nearly thirty years after he stood at that kitchen sink, washing dishes and watching the performance that inspired him to follow his dream, Billy Porter won his own Tony Award for Best Actor in a Musical!

Billy was happy to discover more shows being made with Black characters who were out and proud, like he was.

In 2019, Billy won television's biggest honor, an Emmy Award, for Lead Actor in a Drama Series for his work on *Pose*. The TV show was about a group of LGBTQ+ New Yorkers who love to dance and express themselves.

Next, Billy played Fab G in the 2021 movie musical
Cinderella. The role was all about being fabulous and
spreading love. The movie's writer and director knew
Billy would be the most glamorous fairy godmother of
them all!

Billy always stayed fabulous and fashionable, on and off the stage. When he finally got an invitation to the Oscars, he worked with a famous designer to create the perfect outfit. The top half was a classic tuxedo, like the "boring" suits he used to see. But the bottom half was a beautiful flowing gown.

He had always wanted to use his clothes to make an impression—and that's exactly what he did. Walking down the red carpet in his gorgeous ball gown, Billy felt free.

"When you dare to dream the impossible, impossible dreams do come true."

Billy Porter uses singing, acting, and fashion to encourage everyone to be their true selves. He knows that loving who you are is more important than winning any award.